THE ANCIENT MAYA

BY MADELINE TYLER

KidHaven
PUBLISHING

UNLOCKING ANCIENT CIVILIZATIONS

Published in 2019 by KidHaven Publishing, an Imprint of Greenhaven Publishing, LLC
353 3rd Avenue, Suite 255, New York, NY 10010

This edition is published by arrangement with Booklife Publishing.

Written by: Madeline Tyler
Edited by: Holly Duhig
Designed by: Daniel Scase

Cataloging-in-Publication Data

Names: Tyler, Madeline.
Title: The ancient Maya / Madeline Tyler.
Description: New York : KidHaven Publishing, 2019. | Series: Unlocking ancient civilizations | Includes glossary and index.
Identifiers: ISBN 9781534529038 (pbk.) | ISBN 9781534529052 (library bound) | ISBN 9781534529045 (6 pack) |
ISBN 9781534529069 (ebook)
Subjects: LCSH: Mayas--Juvenile literature. | Mayas--History--Juvenile literature. | Mayas--Social life and customs--
Juvenile literature. | Mayas--Civilization--Juvenile literature.
Classification: LCC F1435.T95 2019 | DDC 972.81--dc23

Printed in the United States of America

CPSIA compliance information: Batch # BW19KL: For further information
contact Greenhaven Publishing LLC, New York, New York at 1-844-317-7404.

PHOTO CREDITS

Front Cover – Lukiyanova Natalia frenta. Front Cover Background – soft_light. 2 – photopixel. 3 – Lukiyanova Natalia frenta. 4 – Johnny Habell, HJPD.
5 – Christian Delbert. 6 – Diego Grandi, Janez Zalaznik. 7 – Simon Dannhauer, Mały koleżka, Svetlana Bykova. 8 – emperorcosar, Liz Stepanoff. 9 –
Diego Grandi. 10 – tato grasso, GTS Productions. 11 – Tortoon. 12 – Nataiki, BestForBest, Elichten. 13 – Anton_Ivanov, W. Scott McGill. 14 – Rafal Cichawa.
15 – Wikipedia, Jeremy Reddington. 16 – BabelStone, Joseph Thomas Photography. 17 – Deborah McCague, Wikicommons. 18 – Ralf Broskvar. 19 –
Leonard G, Simon Burchell, Dorieo. 20 – Alexander von Humboldt, guardiano007. 21 – Peter Hermes Furian. 22 – Milosz Maslanka, Naaman Abreu. 23 –
Jacob Rus, Leon Rafael. 24 – Jess Kraft, Irina Klyuchnikova. 25 – HJPD, Lienzo de Tlaxcala. 26 – Aran1988. 28 & 29 – Pierdelune, DC_Aperture, Capslock,
Yummyphotos, Iurii Kazakov, Milosz Maslanka, ANDREA DELBO, Leon Rafael, Paco Forriol, Nataiki, Lacambalam, Michael Rosskothen, Lienzo de Tlaxcala.
32 – Lukiyanova Natalia frenta

Images are courtesy of Shutterstock.com. With thanks to Getty Images, Thinkstock Photo and iStockphoto.

THE ANCIENT MAYA

CONTENTS

Words that look like *this* are explained in the glossary on page 31.

THE ANCIENT MAYA

THE ancient Maya people were part of a *civilization* in present-day Central America. The Mayan civilization was one of the most important civilizations in the world. The Maya were very advanced mathematicians and *astronomers* who used their knowledge and studies to develop complicated but accurate calendars. They were also experienced in working with stone, and created many buildings and sculptures that can still be seen to this day.

Although people began to form small villages in the Maya region around 4,000 years ago, the Maya civilization did not begin until 1000 *B.C.* This period, which spanned from 2000 B.C. to *A.D.* 250, is called the Preclassic period. The civilization lasted for thousands of years before it started to collapse in around A.D. 800. Unlike other historical civilizations, like the ancient Greek and ancient Roman, the Maya were not part of an *empire*. Instead, each city was *autonomous*. This means that they all had their own ruler and there was no single Maya king.

THE ANCIENT CITY OF ZACULEU, IN PRESENT-DAY GUATEMALA, IS A POPULAR SITE THAT HAS MORE THAN 40 DIFFERENT RUINS.

MESOAMERICA

The Maya civilization was part of Mesoamerica. Mesoamerica is an area of Central America where many civilizations, including the Mayan and Aztec, thrived before Spanish *colonizers* settled there during the 15th and 16th centuries. The *indigenous* people of Mesoamerica shared a similar culture and way of life; they farmed crops such as maize, avocados, cotton, and chili peppers, and *domesticated* animals including dogs and turkeys. They also built temple pyramids and made statues and sculptures to worship their gods.

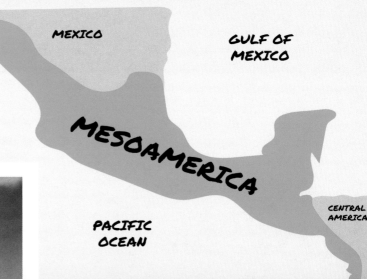

MEXICO

GULF OF MEXICO

MESOAMERICA

PACIFIC OCEAN

CENTRAL AMERICA

EL CASTILLO, OR THE TEMPLE OF KUKULKAN, IS ONE OF THE MOST WELL-KNOWN MAYA PYRAMIDS. IT IS IN THE ANCIENT CITY OF CHICHEN ITZA, IN PRESENT-DAY MEXICO, AND WAS BUILT IN AROUND A.D. 800, DURING THE LATE CLASSIC PERIOD.

SPANISH COLONIZATION

An explorer called Christopher Columbus sailed from Spain to the Americas in 1492. After this, more people from Spain began to settle in North, South, and Central America. They conquered the local people and forced them into *slavery*. Many indigenous people died, and the Spanish colonizers soon took control of the people and their land, making them speak Spanish instead of their own languages.

MAYA CITIES

THIS IS THE ANCIENT CITY OF TIKAL, IN WHAT IS NOW GUATEMALA.

THE Maya had many different cities. The ruins of the cities can be found in Mexico, Guatemala, Belize, and Honduras. Each city had its own king who lived with his family in a grand palace. The king ruled the city, local area, and the people that lived nearby. Maya cities often looked very similar to each other and many of them were built during the Classic period. Most of them had a palace, pyramid temples, a plaza for a marketplace, and a court to play ball games. When the civilization was at its largest, there were more than 40 Maya cities and each city had between 5,000 and 50,000 people living there. Historians have learned a lot about the Maya by studying their cities and buildings.

SOME CITIES, LIKE TULUM, HAD WALLS AROUND THEM. THESE ACTED AS A DEFENSE TO PROTECT THE PEOPLE FROM ENEMY INVASIONS.

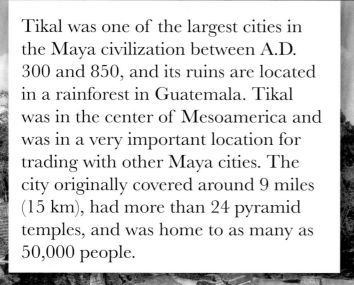

Tikal was one of the largest cities in the Maya civilization between A.D. 300 and 850, and its ruins are located in a rainforest in Guatemala. Tikal was in the center of Mesoamerica and was in a very important location for trading with other Maya cities. The city originally covered around 9 miles (15 km), had more than 24 pyramid temples, and was home to as many as 50,000 people.

Tikal was ruled by a dynasty. A dynasty is a line of rulers who all come from the same family. When a king died, his eldest son became king. If the king had no son, then his eldest brother would replace him as the ruler.

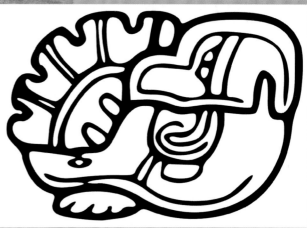

SOME HISTORIANS BELIEVE THAT YAX EHB XOOK WAS THE FIRST KING OF TIKAL AND THE FOUNDER OF ITS DYNASTY. THIS IS HIS *glyph*.

Archaeologists found many huge stelae amongst the Tikal ruins. Stelae are very tall stone sculptures that were often used as gravestones or as a way of celebrating a priest or king and had hieroglyphs and dates carved into them. Hieroglyphs are small pictures that are used to represent a word or sound.

PYRAMIDS AND TEMPLES

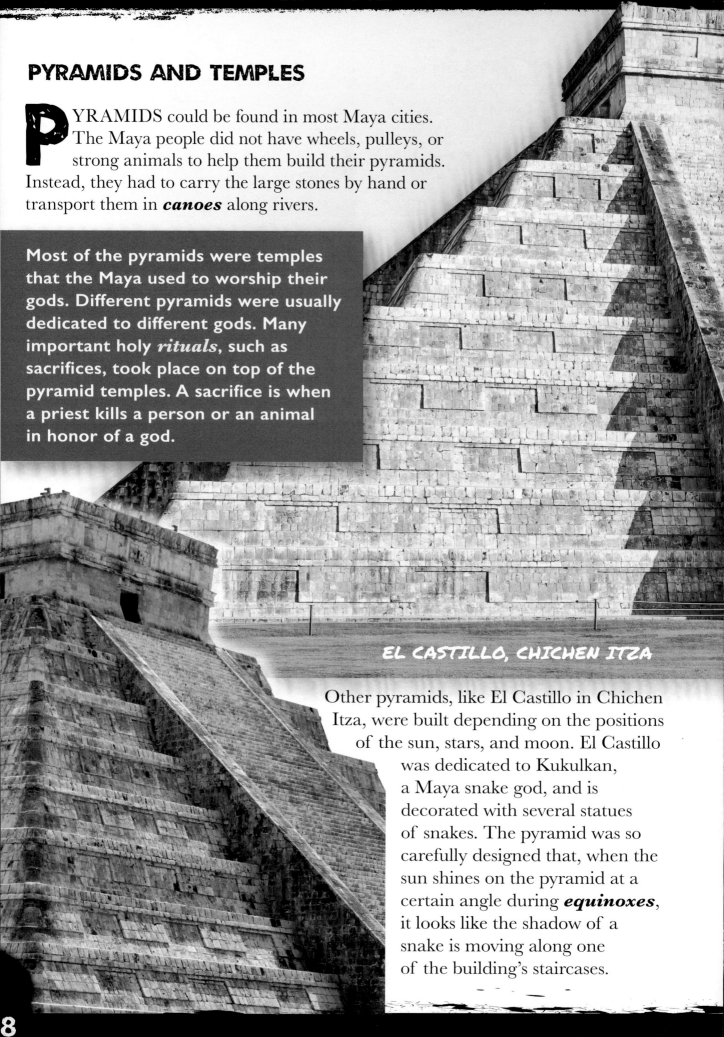

PYRAMIDS could be found in most Maya cities. The Maya people did not have wheels, pulleys, or strong animals to help them build their pyramids. Instead, they had to carry the large stones by hand or transport them in *canoes* along rivers.

Most of the pyramids were temples that the Maya used to worship their gods. Different pyramids were usually dedicated to different gods. Many important holy *rituals*, such as sacrifices, took place on top of the pyramid temples. A sacrifice is when a priest kills a person or an animal in honor of a god.

EL CASTILLO, CHICHEN ITZA

Other pyramids, like El Castillo in Chichen Itza, were built depending on the positions of the sun, stars, and moon. El Castillo was dedicated to Kukulkan, a Maya snake god, and is decorated with several statues of snakes. The pyramid was so carefully designed that, when the sun shines on the pyramid at a certain angle during *equinoxes*, it looks like the shadow of a snake is moving along one of the building's staircases.

MAYA BALL GAME

A type of Mesoamerican ball game was played all through Central America. The game was very important to the Maya people and many cities had a court to play the game on, usually close to the temples. Priests and leaders would watch the games and religious songs were often sung. The winning team would be congratulated and treated like heroes, but the losing team had to face a punishment. The winners received trophies while the captain of the losing team was sometimes killed as part of a human sacrifice to the gods. Dying for the gods was considered a huge honor, so some historians believe that the winning team was sacrificed instead.

Players had to pass the ball between them without using their hands or feet, and try to get the ball through one of the stone rings around the edge of the court. People from all across Maya society played and enjoyed the game.

EVERYDAY LIFE

PALACE OF THE MASKS, KABAH, MEXICO

MAYA SOCIETY

MAYA society was divided into a *hierarchy* with different classes in 300 B.C. The king was at the top and had complete control over the citizens of his city. The priests and nobles were next. They made decisions about how the city was run, how wars were fought, and how to worship the gods. After this came the merchants and artisans. The artisans made sculptures, *murals*, and other works of art to give thanks to the gods. The merchants also traveled between cities trading goods. The *peasants* and farmers came next, while the slaves were part of the very lowest class.

HOMES

The king and his family lived in grand palaces in the center of the city. The palaces were very large and made of stone. They were often used for meetings with other leaders and for celebrations like feasts and dances. The peasants and lower classes lived in small houses towards the outside of the city. Their houses were usually made of wood, stone, or mud and were covered in hay.

THIS IS WHAT THE HOUSE OF A MODERN MAYA FAMILY LOOKS LIKE.

FAMILY LIFE

The Maya people lived with their families in one house. Peasant women had many jobs within the home. It was their responsibility to cook, raise the children, look after the garden, and weave cloth to make clothes. The men and boys went out to work in fields, tending to crops like maize, avocados, and tomatoes. Maya women used the maize to make cornmeal, a type of flour, by grinding the maize into a very fine powder. The cornmeal was then used to make tortillas, which were eaten with every meal.

MAIZE FIELD

FARMING

Farming was an important part of Maya society, and has been for over 2,400 years. Forests were often cleared to make way for more farming land. Water was collected in *sinkholes* and then brought to the fields by using human-made rivers called canals. The Maya grew lots of maize as well as beans, squashes, fruit, and cacao pods. The beans from cacao pods can be used to make chocolate. The Maya used the cacao beans to make a drink similar to present-day hot chocolate. The cacao beans were so precious to the Maya that they used them instead of money to buy things. Other crops were sometimes traded with nearby cities for slaves, salt, metals, shells, and feathers.

CACAO TREES WERE FIRST GROWN IN CENTRAL AND SOUTH AMERICA.

Some Maya were very skilled beekeepers. They raised stingless bees and used the honey as a sweetener and as an *antibiotic*. Beekeeping was important to Maya religion, and a priest would harvest the honey twice a year during a religious ceremony.

nor Lichtenberg

As well as farming, the Maya relied on hunting and fishing, too. They hunted deer, turkeys, monkeys, and ducks with spears and clubs. They ate the meat from the animals and used the skin, fur, and feathers to make clothing. Deer skin was used to make sandals and feathers were used in headdresses. Only the noblemen could use feathers in their clothing, and if a peasant used feathers, they could be killed.

The fishermen used nets and lines in both the rivers and ocean to catch fish. They salted and dried or roasted the fish over an open fire. Sometimes they would cook the fish in a stew with lots of vegetables.

MAYA HUNTING SPEARS AND ARROWHEADS

LANGUAGE AND WRITING

THERE are around 30 different languages spoken by the Maya people today, and many can be traced back almost 4,000 years. The Maya were the first indigenous people in the Americas to develop a writing system to record their language. They began using it around 300 or 200 B.C. and it was made up of over 800 different characters. Some of the characters are hieroglyphs and are drawn as pictures of the things that they represent. Others represent sounds and show you how to say the word. By putting lots of characters together, the Maya wrote about their history, their religion, and the world around them.

MANY OF THE MAYAN LANGUAGES ARE STILL SPOKEN BY INDIGENOUS MAYA PEOPLE IN CENTRAL AMERICA TODAY.

The Maya carved their writing on stelae, sculptures, pottery, and onto the walls of the temples. They wrote about their history and leaders, religious rituals and ceremonies, and astronomy. They also recorded any important events or dates.

CODICES

Priests were very wealthy and were some of the most educated members of Maya society. They were some of the only people that learned to read and write. Mayan priests wrote books called codices. They wrote on sheets of soft tree bark, folded the sheets together, and then covered them in jaguar skin. Only four of these codices still exist today. They are called the Dresden Codex, the Madrid Codex, the Grolier Codex, and the Paris Codex. The Dresden Codex is the oldest and is believed to have been written in around A.D. 1200. The codex contains information on the *phases* of Venus, the *eclipses* of the sun and moon, and calendars that predict the future. Recording information and movements of the moon, the sun, and the planets was very important to the Maya because they believed that the gods were guiding them across the sky.

DRESDEN CODEX

THE DRESDEN CODEX, THE MADRID CODEX, AND THE PARIS CODEX ARE ALL NAMED AFTER THE CITIES THAT THEY WERE REDISCOVERED IN AND ARE NOW KEPT.

There were many more codices, but they were destroyed by Spanish priests during the colonization of the Americas. The priests destroyed them because they disagreed with the writings about Maya gods. They wanted the Maya to abandon their gods and become *Catholics*.

GODS AND RELIGION

RELIGION was central to Maya life and affected nearly everything they did. They believed that humans had been created to honor the gods, so they worshipped them every day and in all parts of life.

BLOODLETTING

Bloodletting was a ritual only the royal family could perform. It was usually done to mark important events such as a birth or an anniversary. Maya kings and queens would use special tools made of stingray spines or obsidian to cut different parts of their body and release blood.

THIS CARVING SHOWS THE MAYAN QUEEN, LADY XOC, CUTTING HER TONGUE WITH A BARBED ROPE.

STONE KNIVES LIKE THESE WERE SOMETIMES USED IN SACRIFICES.

HUMAN SACRIFICE

When the Maya went to war, they would often try to capture prisoners from other cities to be used for sacrifice. They believed that offering sacrifices to the gods was necessary to show their gratitude.

They also believed that the gods would reward them for their offering by giving them a good harvest and helping them win future battles.

DEATH AND BURIALS

The Maya thought being sacrificed to the gods was a great honor. When a Maya person died, they believed that they would be sent straight to the underworld, called Xibalba or Metnal. To get to Tamoanchan, or paradise, they had to cross the nine levels of Xibalba to reach Earth, and then climb 13 more levels. However, the Maya believed that if a person died through sacrifice, childbirth, or war, they went straight to Tamoanchan without being sent to Xibalba first.

THE AZTEC CIVILIZATION ALSO BELIEVED IN A PARADISE CALLED TAMOANCHAN. THESE IMAGES FROM THE CODEX BORGIA SHOW HOW THE AZTECS BELIEVED TAMOANCHAN WOULD LOOK.

The Maya were buried facing west to go to Xibalba, or north to go to Tamoanchan. They were buried with maize in their mouth to feed them on their journey. Finally, they were sprinkled with red *minerals* and wrapped in a cotton cloth.

MAYA LEADERS AND OTHER IMPORTANT FIGURES WERE OFTEN BURIED WITH POTTERY, JADE STATUES, AND MASKS.

THE CREATION STORY

THE Maya believe that Huracán, the wind and sky god, created the Earth. He planted a large ceiba tree to separate the Earth and sky, and make room for plants and animals to grow. The ceiba roots grew into the underworld of Xibalba and the branches stretched up into Tamoanchan.

Next, the gods created animals and plants, but they were not happy. They wanted something that could worship them, so they created four men, and then four women. The Maya believe that the gods created humans by mixing corn with water.

It took the gods three tries to successfully make humans. For the first attempt, the gods made people from mud, but they could not walk. For the second, the gods used wood and reeds, but these people did not worship the gods. Finally, they used corn and water to make the first eight humans.

MAYA GODS

The ancient Maya worshipped lots of different gods. The gods could change to look like either humans or animals. Each god was dedicated to something different in Maya life. Chac is the god of rain, and can produce rain and thunder. The Maya believed that he was covered in scales and had fangs, like a snake. He was very important to the Maya as he brought rain to water their crops and for them to drink. Itzamna is another important god to the Maya. He helped to create humans and taught them how to grow corn, to write, and to use medicine. He is also the god of day and night.

CHAC

MAYAN SUN GOD, KINICH AHAU

Sun worship was important in almost all Mesoamerican religions. The Maya believed that they had to make human sacrifices to the sun god, Kinich Ahau, so that he could continue to move across the sky.

THIS TILE CONTAINS AN IMAGE OF THE GOD ITZAMNA.

MAYA CALENDAR

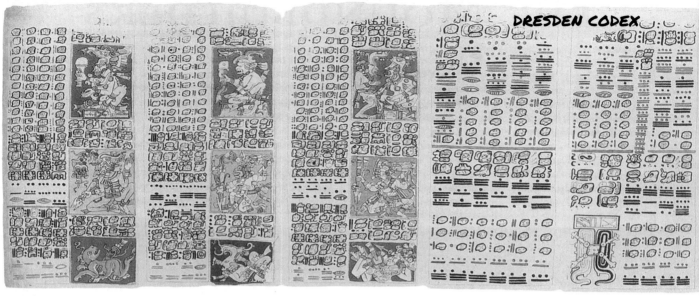

DRESDEN CODEX

THE Maya believed that they could learn more about their gods through astronomy, which is the study of the sun, moon, stars, and planets. They believed that Earth was at the center of the universe and that the gods guided everything else across the sky above them. They watched the movements very carefully so that they knew when to worship the gods, make sacrifices, and even when to go to war. Venus was very important to the Maya, and one ancient Maya astronomer recorded the rising and setting of Venus in the Dresden Codex. By tracking Venus and other objects in the sky, the Maya were able to create a very early calendar. They used this calendar to help track stars and planets and to record the reigns of different rulers and other important dates and events. The calendar helped the Maya to plan their wars to happen as Venus first appeared in the morning sky.

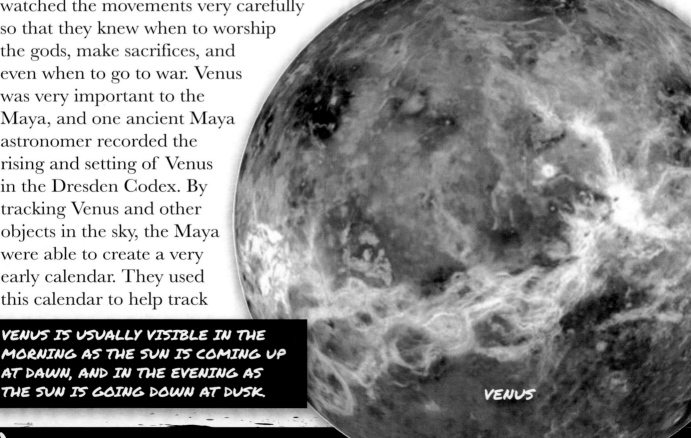

VENUS IS USUALLY VISIBLE IN THE MORNING AS THE SUN IS COMING UP AT DAWN, AND IN THE EVENING AS THE SUN IS GOING DOWN AT DUSK.

VENUS

Although the first Maya calendar was created a very long time ago, it was detailed, complex, and accurate. The Maya calendar was made up of two calendars: the Tzolk'in and the Haab'.

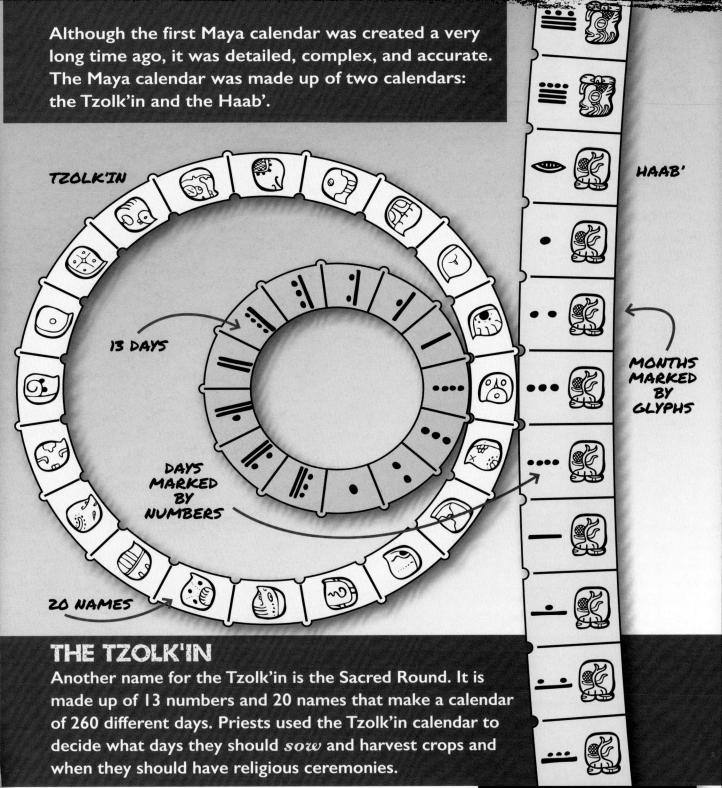

TZOLK'IN

13 DAYS

DAYS MARKED BY NUMBERS

20 NAMES

HAAB'

MONTHS MARKED BY GLYPHS

THE TZOLK'IN

Another name for the Tzolk'in is the Sacred Round. It is made up of 13 numbers and 20 names that make a calendar of 260 different days. Priests used the Tzolk'in calendar to decide what days they should *sow* and harvest crops and when they should have religious ceremonies.

The Haab' calendar is based on the sun. It is made up of 18 months that all have 20 days. At the end of the year, there is a short, unlucky month of only five days, called Wayeb. The Maya used the number and name from the Tzolk'in calendar, and the number and glyph from the Haab' to record the day of the year. The day would not be repeated for 52 years. This is called a Calendar Round.

THE MAYA ALSO USED A THIRD CALENDAR, CALLED THE LONG COUNT CALENDAR. THIS COUNTS EVERY DAY SINCE THE 11TH OF AUGUST, 2114 B.C. EACH CYCLE OF THE LONG COUNT CALENDAR HAS 5,125 DAYS.

ART AND CULTURE

Different artworks can be seen throughout the Maya civilization. The Maya carved sculptures and stelae, painted murals, and made ceramic pottery like plates and bowls. They also made clothing and headdresses by weaving fabrics and using feathers. Some pieces of art were religious and were designed to look nice, and others had a specific purpose, like holding food and drink or keeping the Maya warm.

SCULPTURES

The Maya made many sculptures by carving designs into stone, wood, and a mineral called jade. They carved stelae to honor the gods and they were often dedicated to the king. They were carved with images of a god or a king, and had hieroglyphs that described their life and achievements. The people who made the sculptures were sculptors. They used wooden mallets and stone tools to carve their designs.

MAYA HIEROGLYPH CARVED INTO STONE

PAINTING

The Maya painted murals on the walls of their houses and temples. The paintings would usually show scenes of daily life, battle, or important parts of the Maya religion.

MANY OF THE MURALS HAVE FADED, AND THE IMAGES ARE NOT AS CLEAR ANYMORE. SOME HISTORIANS AND ARCHAEOLOGISTS BELIEVE THAT THIS MAY BE WHAT THE ORIGINAL MURALS LOOKED LIKE.

The Templo de las Pinturas, or Temple of Paintings, at Bonampak, Mexico, was built in A.D. 790 and is decorated with colorful mural paintings. They tell stories related to the Maya leader Chan Muwaan II's rule, showing important events such as royal ceremonies, battles, and religious rituals like sacrifices and bloodletting. The murals have taught historians a lot about what life was like in the Maya civilization. By studying the murals, they have been able to learn about what clothes the different classes wore, what food they ate, and how they prepared it.

THE END OF THE ANCIENT MAYA

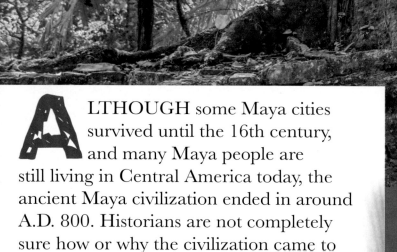

ALTHOUGH some Maya cities survived until the 16th century, and many Maya people are still living in Central America today, the ancient Maya civilization ended in around A.D. 800. Historians are not completely sure how or why the civilization came to an end, but they believe that there are several factors that led to its collapse.

The ancient Maya cleared areas of rainforest to make space for settlements and to grow crops like maize. They also needed the wood from the trees as fuel for fires to cook their food and prepare the lime plaster used to build their pyramids and homes. As the cities grew, more trees needed to be chopped down and more forest had to be cleared away. This may have caused the land to become *barren*, so crops could no longer be grown there. Anyone who did not move to a new settlement would have probably died from *starvation*.

AFTER THE MAYA ABANDONED THEIR CITIES, THE RAINFOREST BEGAN TO GROW BACK. IT COVERED LOTS OF THE BUILDINGS AND SOME OF THE CITIES WERE HIDDEN FOR HUNDREDS OF YEARS.

When the Spanish invaders arrived in the Americas in 1492, it soon led to a long period of colonization. Colonization is when people travel to a different country or area and take control of the land and its people, usually with force. Although most of the Maya civilization had already disappeared by this time, there were still some Maya villages in the rainforests. However, the Spanish colonizers took control of these villages and treated the people very cruelly. They killed a lot of the indigenous populations of the Americas, including Maya, Aztec, and Inca people, and made many others slaves.

LIENZO DE TLAXCALA

THE LIENZO DE TLAXCALA WAS MADE BY THE TLAXCALTEC PEOPLE, WHO FOUGHT ALONGSIDE THE SPANISH COLONIZERS IN MEXICO AGAINST THE MAYA, ZAPOTEC, AND MIXTEC PEOPLE. THE LIENZO SHOWS SOME OF THESE BATTLES.

A GROUP OF MAYA CALLED THE K'ICHE' WERE DEFEATED BY THE SPANISH AT UTATLÁN. AT THE TIME, UTATLÁN WAS ONE OF THE MOST POWERFUL MAYA CITIES.

The colonizers also brought with them new, European diseases like smallpox and measles that the people of Mesoamerica had never been in contact with before. The Maya were not immune, which means that their bodies did not protect them against the diseases. Many of the Maya died from these diseases, and their population became even smaller.

THE LEGACY OF THE ANCIENT MAYA

MAYA achievements and the legacy of their civilization can be seen in many parts of modern life today. The Maya were very advanced astronomers, mathematicians, and engineers, and were also one of the first civilizations to develop a writing system.

THE MAYA MADE RUBBER BY MIXING LATEX WITH THE JUICE FROM MORNING GLORY VINES. BY USING DIFFERENT AMOUNTS OF EACH INGREDIENT, THEY COULD MAKE THE RUBBER MORE OR LESS BOUNCY.

RUBBER

Rubber is a stretchy and waterproof material that is made by using a type of *sap* called latex from the rubber tree. Rubber can be used to make shoes, tires, balls, and balloons. Historians believe that the Maya used latex to make rubber over 3,000 years ago. They used the rubber to bind their books together and to make balls, glue, and waterproof cloth.

MATHEMATICS AND ZERO

As well as developing glyphs for words and sounds, the Maya also used symbols to stand for different numbers: a dot stood for the number one, and a horizontal line represented the number five. Each symbol had a different *value* and, when put together in different orders, could represent a different number. They used these numbers in their calendars and carved them into stelae to record dates. Mathematics was very important to the Maya, as they used it in astronomy and in constructing large buildings like pyramids.

MAYAN POSITIONAL NUMBER SYSTEM

They were some of the first people to use zero in their number system. A shell shape was used as the symbol for zero. They used it in calculations and to show that numbers like "2" and "20" or "51" and "501" have different values. In contrast, the ancient Greeks and Romans did not have a symbol to represent zero, and the number did not arrive in Europe until around A.D. 1200.

TIMELINE OF THE

2000 B.C.

PEOPLE BEGIN TO SETTLE IN SMALL VILLAGES

2000 B.C.

THE PRECLASSIC PERIOD BEGINS

600 B.C.
THE MAYA BEGIN FARMING

300 - 200 B.C.
THE MAYA DEVELOP A WRITING SYSTEM

A.D. 790

THE TEMPLE OF PAINTINGS IS BUILT AND DECORATED

A.D. 800

THE MAYA CIVILIZATION BEGINS TO COLLAPSE

A.D. 950

THE POST-CLASSIC PERIOD BEGINS

ANCIENT MAYA

100 B.C.

THE FIRST MAYA PYRAMIDS ARE BUILT

A.D. 300

THE CLASSIC PERIOD BEGINS

A.D. 300-850

TIKAL IS BUILT AND BECOMES AN IMPORTANT MAYA CITY

A.D. 1200

THE DRESDEN CODEX IS WRITTEN

A.D. 1492

CHRISTOPHER COLUMBUS SAILS TO THE AMERICAS

A.D. 1517

THE SPANISH ARRIVE IN MAYA LANDS

MAP OF THE ANCIENT MAYA

GULF OF
MEXICO

CANCUN

CHICHEN ITZA

UXMAL

COBA

CAMPECHE

TULUM

MEXICO

BECAN

PALENQUE

TIKAL

BELMOPAN

BONAMPAK

BELIZE

CARIBBEAN
SEA

GUATEMALA

HONDURAS

COPAN

GUATEMALA

SAN SALVADOR

EL SALVADOR

NORTH PACIFIC OCEAN

NICARAGUA

MAYA AREA

GLOSSARY

A.D.	"in the year of the lord", marks the time after Christians believe Jesus was born
antibiotic	a substance that stops germs and other small living things from growing
archaeologists	historians who study buried ruins and ancient objects in order to learn about human history
astronomers	people who study the universe and objects in space
autonomous	somewhere that is free and independent and rules itself
barren	unable to produce or support the growth of crops
B.C.	meaning "before Christ", it is used to mark dates that occurred before Christians believe Jesus was born
canoes	narrow boats that are moved using a paddle
Catholics	a group of Christians who are led by the pope
civilization	a society that is very advanced
colonizers	people who move to a new land to take control of the area and people
domesticated	referring to an animal that is tamed so that it can be kept by humans
eclipses	when a planet, star, or moon is hidden by another, or by a shadow
empire	a group of countries or nations under one ruler
equinoxes	two times a year when the day and night are 12 hours long everywhere in the world
glyph	a picture that represents a word or sound
hierarchy	a system where people are ranked in order of power, status, or authority
indigenous	originating or naturally found in a particular place
minerals	natural, useful, and sometimes valuable substances, often obtained from rocks in the ground
murals	artwork painted directly onto walls
peasants	poor land workers who belonged to the lowest social class
phases	a stage in a moon or planet's cycle of phases; how much of a moon or planet is visible by being lit by the sun
rituals	ordered actions that take place during religious ceremonies
sap	liquid that carries water and nutrients to the parts of a plant
sinkholes	hollow places in the earth where water collects
slavery	the state of being owned by another person and having no freedom
sow	to plant in the ground
starvation	suffering or death caused by lack of food
value	the worth of something

INDEX